This book is dedicated to my daughter Aya who started traveling the world when she was 6 weeks old, and to my husband Justin who makes these travels possible.

Nick, Aya and their parents Kate and George are traveling to Argentina for a family vacation. It is winter in the United States, and summer in the Southern Hemisphere.

They board a non-stop flight in Miami and 9 hours later land in Buenos Aires.

Buenos Aires is the capital city of Argentina and it has many places of interest to explore. The family visits the Plaza de Mayo and goes on a tour to Casa Rosada, the seat of the country's government. There are officers on standing duty there, and Nick is fascinated with their uniforms.

Aya has been learning numbers and colors. She has never seen such a pretty pink building before. She is standing outside and counting windows, including the ones on the roof. How many did you count? She saw 42!

Then Aya notices a flag and asks, "Daddy, what does this flag mean?"
"The baby blue color represents the sky, the white symbolizes clouds and yellow is the sun in the middle," her father explains.

At the end of the day, they visit a neighborhood called La Boca and take a walk at the street called Caminito. Aya immediately starts naming all the colors she sees while pointing at the buildings. "Purple, blue, turquoise, yellow, red, orange! Wow, these buildings are so bright and colorful!"

CLUB ATLÉTICO
BOCA JUNIORS

"My friend told me that the famous football team Boca Juniors comes from this area. I have to go see their stadium," says Nick. "Ok, we will all walk to the stadium before dinner," responds his mother.

After a few days at the capital, the family takes a domestic flight to Bariloche, a city located southwest of Buenos Aires, near the border with Chile. They go to the museum of artisan crafts and buy candies in chocolate stores on the main street. They take a photo with a Saint Bernard dog on the plaza by the Civic Center. It is believed that in the past, these dogs, bearing a neck barrel filled with liquid, rescued people who were lost in the mountains.

Before leaving Bariloche, Nick, Aya and their parents ride in a cable car to the mountain overlooking beautiful Lake Nahuel Huapi and the surrounding countryside.

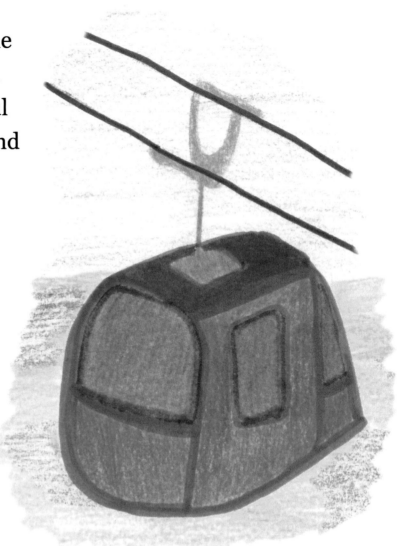

The four travelers rent a camper van and head south to explore Patagonia. Driving on the famous road Ruta 40, they see purple and pink flowers covering the foothills of the mountains. "Let's gather these blooming flowers. Purple is my favorite color," says Aya. Soon the girl is holding a big bouquet of lupines in her arms.

They visit the small towns of El Bolsón and Trevelin and Los Alerces National Park along the way. They try traditional Argentine food and deserts, such as EMPANADAS and ALFAJORES and enjoy drinking MATE, the famous gourd-tea of Argentina.

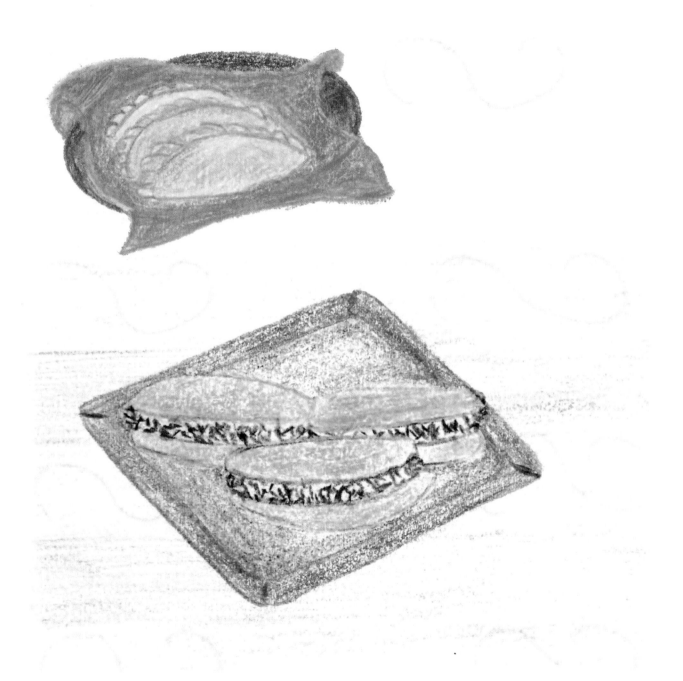

Nick's dream is to go fly-fishing and to catch a big brook trout in one of the pristine streams of Patagonia. His dream becomes a reality when they reach the mouth of the Corcovado River which flows out of Lago Vintter very close to the border with Chile.

While Nick with his father George are fishing, Aya and her mother Kate gather CALAFATE berries from the bushes that surround them. CALAFATE is a plant with sharp thorns and delicious berries that is native to the region of Patagonia in Chile and Argentina.

Continuing south on Ruta 40, the family travels through the Province of Chubut and into Santa Cruz Province. They camp by beautiful lakes, streams and rivers next to the Andes Mountains. One evening a GUANACO, a wild relative of the lama, comes very close to their tent to say hello! "We don't even need to go to a zoo or botanical garden to see so many cool things!" exclaims Nick.

The next day, they see the PAMPA, which is very dry open grassland with herds of sheep and cows. A nomadic horseman known as a GAUCHO, with dog by his side, watches the animals.

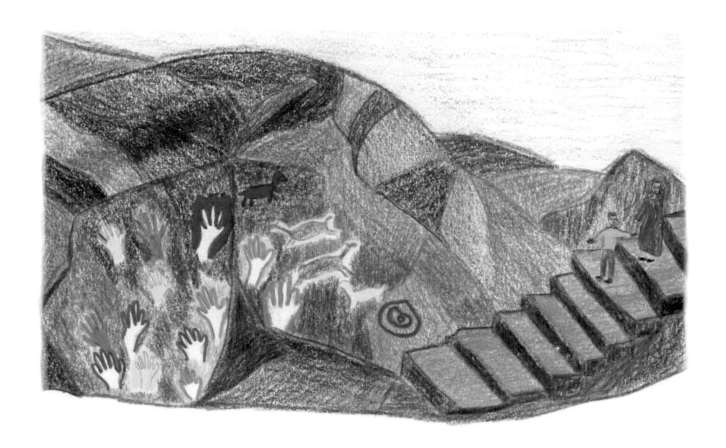

"And now we are entering a place called the Cave of Hands.
The walls of this cave have paintings of animals and birds,
and imprints of people's hands which were made as early
as 9000 years ago," explains mom.
"Thousands of years is a lot of time. I cannot imagine what
the world looked like back then," says Nick.

"You already caught a trout and we saw a guanaco and the cave. I want to see colorful birds," declares Aya. "Flamingos are waiting for us in Laguna Nimez!" her father assures her.

Laguna Nimez Nature Reserve is an important bird sanctuary with over 80 species of birds. People come from all over the world to see the flamingos in the lagoon.

Another destination in Patagonia is the Perito Moreno Glacier in Los Glaciares National Park, and this place is the most impressive to Nick and Aya. Nick takes a piece of ice and while holding it in his hands he says, "these drops of water existed thousands and thousands of years ago and now I am holding them in a form of ice!"

After El Calafate they visit Ushuaia, the southernmost city on Earth, which is located in the Province of Tierra del Fuego. Tierra del Fuego is also an island separated from the mainland by the Strait of Magellan.

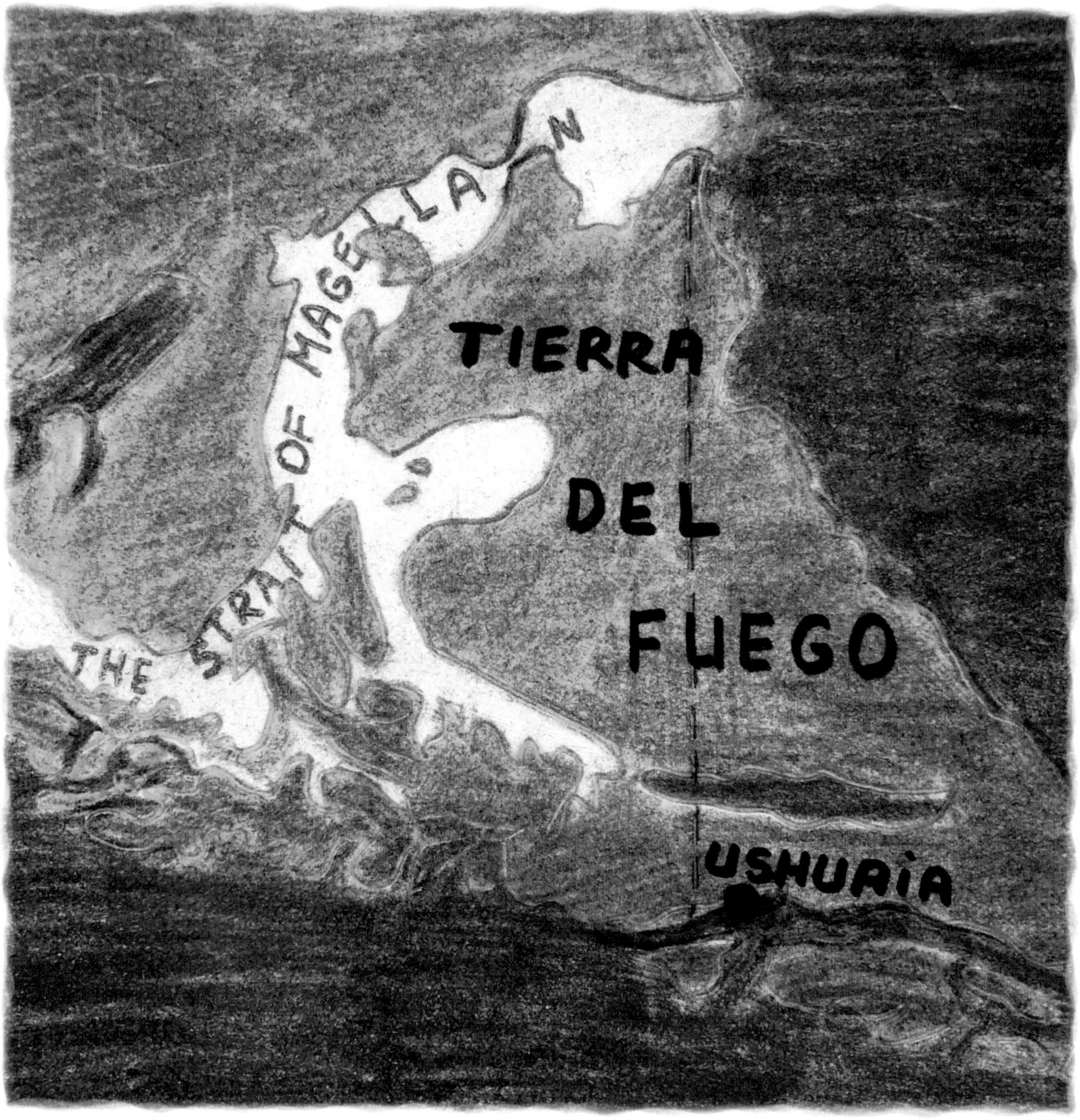
THE STRAIT OF MAGELLAN
TIERRA DEL FUEGO
USHURIA

"Aren't we supposed to see penguins somewhere not far from here?" asks Nick. "Yes, from Ushuaia we will take a boat tour to Martillo Island. We will be able not only to see the Magellanic Penguins from the boat, but also walk next to them!" explains Kate.

In Ushuaia, they return their rented minivan and board a flight to the Iguazu Falls, the largest waterfall system in the world. "There is a lot of water in this river!" exclaims Aya. "Yes! The Iguazu River and the falls separate Argentina from Brazil. I learned this in one of my classes," says Nick.

After Iguazu, Nick, Aya and their parents travel back to the United States. They have so many stories to tell their friends and relatives about everything they saw during their journey through Argentina!

Made in United States
Orlando, FL
02 February 2024